Decluttering Your Kitchen in 5 Easy Steps

Cutting Edge Strategies to Declutter, Clean and Organize Your Kitchen Without the Stress

Lisa Hedberg

© Copyright 2022 - All rights reserved.

The content contained within this book may not be reproduced, duplicated, or transmitted without direct written permission from the author or the publisher.

Under no circumstances will any blame or legal responsibility be held against the publisher, or author, for any damages, reparation, or monetary loss due to the information contained within this book, either directly or indirectly. You are responsible for your own choices, actions, and results.

Legal Notice:

This book is copyright protected. This book is only for personal use. You cannot amend, distribute, sell, use, quote or paraphrase any part, or the content within this book, without the consent of the author or publisher.

Disclaimer Notice:

Please note the information contained within this document is for educational and entertainment purposes only. All effort has been executed to present accurate, up to date, and reliable, complete information. No warranties of any kind are declared or implied. Readers acknowledge that the author is not engaging in the rendering of legal, financial, medical, or professional advice. The content within this book has been derived from various sources. Please consult a licensed professional before attempting any techniques outlined in this book.

By reading this document, the reader agrees that under no circumstances is the author responsible for any losses, direct or indirect, which are incurred as a result of the use of the information contained within this document, including, but not limited to, errors, omissions, or inaccuracies.

Your Free Gift

As a way of saying thanks for your purchase, I'm offering the eBook, *7 Tips to Declutter Your Life* and the *Decluttering Workbook* for FREE to my readers.

To get instant access, just go to:
http://publishingdove.com/

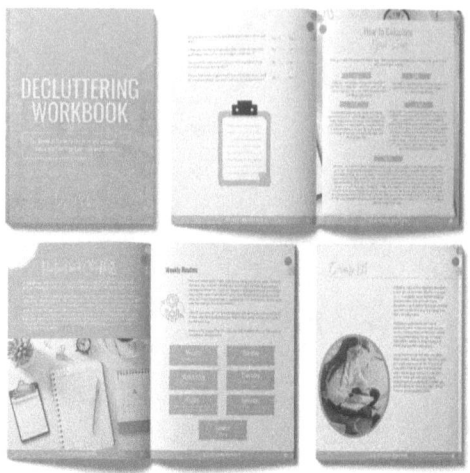

Inside the free download, you will discover:

- A printable format of all the exercises and checklists from the book, *Decluttering Workbook: The Essential Guide to Organize and Declutter Your Home With Exercises and Checklists*

- A colorful, stunning, and eye-catching exercise and checklist design

And you will have the option to write in, cut out, and hang or pin the printable worksheets however you like!

Inside the eBook, you will discover:

- Decluttering tools that will save you hours on decluttering your home.
- The secret decluttering techniques that the experts swear by.
- Authentic views, relatable advice, and a fruitful and wholesome decluttering experience from an author who has been in a similar position as you before.
- How to avoid a messy home and even messier thoughts with this book that will guide you through the journey of decluttering your living space and your life.
- And so much more!

If you want to live a happier, healthier life and look forward to coming home every day, make sure to grab your free eBook.

"Clutter is not just the stuff on your floor – it's anything that stands between you and the life you want to be living."

— *Peter Walsh*

Introduction

Your kitchen is the lung of your house. The rest of the house cannot breathe properly if the kitchen is cluttered and disorganized. Now, I am not suggesting that you should aim to have one of those picture-perfect kitchens from home decor magazines. Your kitchen is not a static space meant for aesthetic pleasure alone. It is a dynamic living space that performs one of the most essential functions of the human experience – the noble task of nourishing you and your family.

If you are like most people, then your kitchen is also a space where a lot of life happens. Maybe you help your kids out with their homework on the dining table, you make plans for the next day, and perhaps, in winters, your family hangs out a lot there since it is so comforting to breathe in the aroma of warm food cooking.

Even if all you ever do in this special space of your home is cook the occasional meal, your kitchen should be a pleasure to work in. It should motivate and inspire you (and your family) to cook healthy meals. When you are in a disorga-

Introduction

nized and cluttered kitchen, it is hard to find anything in time. You get frustrated, scurrying around to find one ingredient after another. This ends up doubling or even tripling your total cooking time. Next time when you are hungry, you feel petrified at the idea of going through the same process all over again. It feels a lot simpler and easier to just order take-out.

Sound like you?

You have my full empathy. I was exactly like you. I thought I hated cooking, but the truth was I just hated cooking in a chaotic kitchen. If you dread the idea of preparing another home-cooked meal, I would challenge you to revisit that assumption once you have decluttered and organized your kitchen.

I want you to have a kitchen that makes you feel nourished and inspired every time you step into it. It should be functional enough to reduce cooking time to the minimum. Trust me, it really doesn't take that long to prepare healthy, wholesome meals for yourself and your family when you know exactly where everything is in your kitchen.

Once you get rid of the excess, it also becomes easier to keep the kitchen looking neat and clean. In this book, I will share with you my very best strategies for decluttering and organizing the kitchen. I will also share with you a cleaning and tidying schedule that is simple and easy to follow.

At this point, it may seem impossible that you'll ever be able to transform your kitchen. But I can promise you that if you implement everything I am sharing in this book, then you WILL definitely get the results. My kitchen was so bad that I could not set foot in it without risking slipping on bottle

Introduction

openers, cereal boxes, or empty food cans that had been lying around for days. If I can do it, then so can you. I believe in you. All I am asking for is that you take the chance and trust me with this – by the time you're done with this book, your kitchen and how you feel about it will have transformed completely (provided you follow all the instructions and do the work!). I am giving you this guarantee – all you have to do is put into practice everything I am teaching you here.

You deserve a beautiful and organized kitchen that is a delight to be in! So let us get started without any further ado!

Chapter 1

Assessing and Planning

"By failing to prepare, you are preparing to fail."

— Benjamin Franklin (Brainy Quote, n.d.)

It doesn't matter whether you are a master chef or not; your kitchen is still one of the most important spaces in your home. In most cases, the kitchen functions as the hub of the house. It is where family members come together not just to feed their bellies but to nourish their souls as well. Irrespective of the physical size of the space available to you, your kitchen should be warm and inviting.

You may be getting the urge to skip this chapter altogether and get straight to the decluttering part but hold your horses! As Brian Tracy says, "Every minute you spend in planning saves 10 minutes in execution; this gives you a 1,000 percent Return on Energy!"

I am not the most patient person in the world, so, just like you, I often just want to get to the task instead of wasting any time on planning and strategizing. Over the years, I have learned that I end up exerting myself, but it's often not especially rewarding – I simply wasn't sufficiently organized. Without proper planning, your energies are not well directed and focused enough to achieve the goal. In fact, you may not even have enough clarity about the goal itself that you are trying to achieve.

I would highly recommend that you do all the exercises suggested in this chapter. Don't do them mentally but write them down on paper or digitally. I personally prefer to use a physical journal for these kinds of tasks as I find it easier to gain clarity on a subject when I am using an actual pen and paper. But even digitally is fine. You just need to put everything in writing, so you have a concrete plan to look at and follow. It will help you enormously as you go through the process of decluttering and reorganizing your kitchen.

Understand How Your Space is Used

In modern times, the kitchen is hardly ever used for just cooking. Think about it – your friend comes over to say hello. You offer to make her a steaming cup of hot chocolate. As you step inside the kitchen, she follows you to help you out but also because you are both wrapped in an interesting conversation. Before you know it, you've already spent several hours in the kitchen talking, discussing, and laughing together over a cup of hot chocolate.

There is a very special kind of drawing power that the kitchen has. It often compels families to huddle together thanks to the enveloping warmth and comfort it provides.

If you are a mother, perhaps you help your kids with their homework at the kitchen table while you are cooking. Maybe you live alone but the kitchen is where you find yourself working on your laptop or working through your finances. It's also possible that the kitchen is where you often sit down to make all your personal and professional phone calls.

While growing up, I often saw my father sitting at the kitchen table balancing checkbooks while talking to my mom. I remember bringing my broken toys to him and he would help me glue them together at the kitchen table.

The point I am trying to make here is that you must have a realistic understanding of how your kitchen is currently being used. Is it a space reserved exclusively for cooking occasional or regular meals (that's hardly ever the case), or does it function as the central hub of your dwelling?

How your kitchen is being used is going to be unique to you and your family. It is crucial that you develop a realistic understanding of it in order to plan this space well. Your kitchen should be aesthetically pleasing, functionally optimized, and efficient to run. Most importantly, it should serve you and your family's unique needs.

Exercise

Write down the answers to the following questions as honestly and realistically as possible. In other words, don't write what you wish were true for your kitchen but what is actually true for your kitchen at the moment. You can also ask these questions to your family members and ask for their input.

- How much time do you spend in your kitchen on an average day?

- How much time does the rest of your family spend in the kitchen on an average day?
- Is your kitchen used exclusively for cooking, or is it used for performing other activities as well? If it's a hub for other activities, then create a list of exactly what kind of things you and your family do in the kitchen.

Understanding the Space You Have Available to You

You can efficiently and aesthetically organize a space only when you understand it. Large and small are relative terms – what may be small for your large family could be a generously large kitchen space for a family of two. So I want you to assess the kind of space you have available to yourself. Is it big enough to meet all your needs, or does it feel too small and cluttered for everything you do there?

From my perspective, decluttering isn't something that is performed merely by eliminating unnecessary objects from a space. I feel it also involves eliminating things that are not relevant to that space. For instance, if you have too many books and notebooks lying on a kitchen table, it can make your space look cluttered. You can make your kitchen more organized instantly by removing those books and notebooks. You could easily shift them to another space that might be more suitable for studying. However, it depends on your situation. If you are a busy mother of two who wants to multitask to use her time most efficiently, then helping your kids with their homework while you're cooking is one of the best ways of doing it. If that's the case, you'll have to think about how you can utilize the kitchen space optimally.

A space looks cluttered when it has objects unintentionally lying around that don't seem to be truly 'at home' there. For instance, a kitchen table used as a desktop is likely to make the kitchen look cluttered because the kitchen table is meant for a completely different activity. A lot of people who must do their desk work in the kitchen end up installing a proper desk and computer in one corner of the kitchen. You can consider this solution if it seems important to be able to perform such tasks in the kitchen.

Now, I want you to try something else out – try getting rid of everything that doesn't actually belong in the kitchen and look at how much space you have available. Does your kitchen feel large and spacious, or do you get the feeling that it is bursting at the seams?

I want you to have a good understanding of your starting point – this will help identify your problem areas. You'll understand better exactly which aspects of your kitchen are bothering you the most and need to be addressed urgently.

Exercise

If you remove everything that doesn't actually belong in the kitchen and assess what you are left with, I would strongly recommend that you start by taking pictures of your kitchen. Do that before anything else. It will assist, not just as a reference for 'before' the makeover appearance, but also because photographing a space often helps us identify problem areas and issues that we otherwise miss.

Write down the answers to the following questions:

- What is the feeling that you get as soon as you enter your kitchen?
- Does your kitchen feel large and spacious or small and suffocating?
- Do you think you have too many visible things lying around? Are there too few? Or, perhaps, there are just enough?
- Which items are occupying the maximum amount of space in your kitchen? Do you and/or your family actually use these items? If yes, then how often are those items used?
- Does your kitchen require additional shelving units/drawers/organizers?
- What is bothering you most about your kitchen now?
- What do you think would be the best way of solving that problem, or what kind of solution would you most prefer for resolving that issue?

Visualize Your Space

Now is the time to start thinking about what you would like your kitchen to look and feel like. Remember, there is no right or wrong answer to this. If you want to work out of your kitchen table eight hours a day, that's totally fine. I am just suggesting that your kitchen space should be used intentionally and efficiently. So if you will be doing a lot of desk work, then as I suggested earlier, it would be best to get a compact but proper computer table installed in one corner.

Similarly, if your family spends a lot of time hanging out in the kitchen, then you can think of ways in which you can make it cozier, more relaxing and comfortable. Perhaps what you need more than anything are chairs that are truly comfortable?

You are the only person (and your family) who would know what works best for your kitchen.

Another important thing that you should do is measure each area before you begin working with it. This is a tip I learned from an interior designer many years ago. I had bought a couch that wouldn't go through the door of my apartment. My interior designer friend enlightened me about the importance of measuring your space before buying any new furniture or, for that matter, any item that will be occupying the space.

I would strongly recommend that you measure your kitchen to see how much actual space you have available to you. A self-retraction metal tape works best for getting accurate measurements. This exercise is going to come in handy in the organizing chapter when we will devise a plan for efficiently organizing your kitchen. For now, I just want you to get a general idea of how big or small your kitchen is by measuring the four sides of it.

Once you have developed a deeper understanding of the size of your kitchen, the next step is to create a vision for what you want it to look like. I advise you to follow the next exercise to assist you with this step.

Exercise

- Measure the four walls of the kitchen to get an idea of the overall space that is available to you.
- Look for images online of kitchens that are spatially

similar to yours and observe how they have been organized.
- Collect images that inspire you – you can pin them to your Pinterest board or store them in an offline folder. You could also print them for inspiration.

Answer the following questions to develop greater clarity about what you would like your kitchen to look and feel like:

- What are the important tasks that I would continue to perform in my kitchen?
- What kind of feeling do I want my kitchen to evoke in me (and in my family members) every time I walk into it? (For instance, should it feel spacious, airy, or warm and cozy?)
- What kind of colors would I like to use in my kitchen?
- Which decor do I like best for my kitchen? (For instance, modern or vintage, classic or mid-century) If you aren't sure what this means, just look for images with the search term 'kitchen design style.'

Chapter 2

Decluttering the Kitchen

"The first step in crafting the life you want is to get rid of everything you don't."

— *Joshua Becker (Goodreads, n.d.)*

As I said in the previous chapter, the kitchen is often the hub of a home. It is where we spend a lot of time, whether cooking, conversing, or doing a host of other things. It's also one area of the house that is likely to become cluttered very quickly – thanks to the many cabinets and drawers most modern kitchens are equipped with.

The kitchen is also one place where we go a step further to justify hoarding different objects we don't really need. I mean, for instance, I counted a total of ten bottle openers when I was regularly reaching out for just one of the ten. Also, very often, our kitchen is designed and equipped with things we wish we were using but that aren't relevant to our current lifestyle. For example, I had a coffee maker occupying valuable real estate on my kitchen countertop when I hadn't had coffee in over a decade.

The process of decluttering isn't just a superficial attempt to rid our life of excesses – it is also a significant process of getting to know ourselves at a much deeper level. You can't declutter without understanding who you are and what your needs are. Of course, the same applies to understanding the needs and personalities of your family members if you are living with them.

When you are decluttering, you aren't just deciding what to keep and what to discard – you are also delving deeper into who you are and the life that you are leading. The better you understand yourself, the easier it is to declutter. According to a November 2020 Harvard study (Hicks, 2020), decluttering can contribute to feelings of well-being.

Four Boxes for the Decluttering Process

For the decluttering process, I strongly advise my clients to get four large cardboard boxes. Label each of them as:

Discard, Donate, Ponder, Fix

In the 'discard' box, you would place all the things that need to be discarded. Since there may be a lot of pantry items like expired food, you want to complete the discarding process as quickly as possible. Don't wait till the box is overflowing. The decluttering process may take you one day, or you could end up needing several days for it. There is nothing wrong with taking longer to complete the decluttering process. Just make sure that you empty the contents of this discard box every day, or at least that should be the ideal you aim for.

Decluttering Your Kitchen in 5 Easy Steps

The 'donate' box would contain items that aren't useful to you but which can be used by someone else. Again, as you are placing items in this box, you can decide mentally where and to whom you want to donate those items. If you want to donate the items to different people or at different locations, you can group the items together and place them in different plastic bags. Label them appropriately so you know which bag is meant for whom.

The third box, which I want you to label as 'ponder,' is part of what I like to call my Command-Z solution. If you have read my other books, then you must already be familiar with it. But for the uninitiated, here is a quick description of what goes in this box. This box would contain all those items that you are currently not using but you're also not ready to part with. It is like hitting command-z on your computer. If, at any point, you feel you are missing any of the items you have placed inside this box, you go back and rescue it. Hence, the discarding process can easily be undone if the need arises. Most of the time, I have found that I hardly remember the items I've placed in this box. Barring a few times, I've hardly ever rescued anything as part of the command-z solution.

I am quite sure you won't miss most of the items you place in this box. After a while, you can go through the items in there and discard and donate all the things that no longer serve you. If you really want to reacquire something back, then you can do so without guilt, as well. The only caveat is that you can do it only when you are truly missing the item. Don't rescue the items when you are going through everything and deciding whether they should be discarded, donated, or saved.

The fourth box would include all those items that you aren't ready to part with, but you also aren't able to use as they are not in a working condition. You are going to put only those items in this box that you intend to get fixed and then start using again. For every item you put into this box, I want you to also create a deadline for when you are going to get it fixed. Otherwise, you'll just be holding on to clutter.

Make note of each item you have put in there by writing the details in a diary (physical or digital), and then assign a deadline by which you must get it fixed. If you forget about the date or just don't end up getting it fixed for one reason or another (like if you realized it is actually beyond repair now), then you must discard that item immediately!

How to Decide What to Keep and What to Discard

Deciding what to keep and what to discard is quite simple – you keep what is useful to you and discard or donate what is not. Now, for kitchen items, this can be quite tricky. You can easily convince yourself that you may want to eat that breakfast granola that's been sitting on the shelf unopened for the last month. You have found another brand of granola that tastes a lot better, and now it seems hard to go back to the old one. But since you have spent money on it, you keep telling yourself that you'll eat it at some point, although there is no timeline for when that elusive 'some day' may arrive.

For most of the kitchen items, I have created a simple rule. I keep only those items that I am currently using or that I intend to use within three months. This rule works best for pantry items as food that is left unattended too often either develops worms or goes bad. In case of other kitchen items such as baking trays or other tools that end up being used once or twice a year, you can extend the timeline. I would still say that if you won't be using something within a year, you most likely don't need that thing. If you haven't used something in the last two years, then chances are you won't be using it any time soon.

Also, decluttering your kitchen can't be a one-off event. You have to regularly keep going through the items stocked up in your kitchen and decide whether they are serving a purpose or not. The kitchen is one of those areas of the house that is likely to become cluttered again right after you have decluttered it. That's why chapter one was so important. To prevent and tackle clutter on a regular basis, you need to have a good understanding of the vision you have for your kitchen and the lifestyle that you are currently leading.

Tackle One Area at a Time

You want to be able to maintain a relatively functional kitchen even while you are decluttering the space. Therefore, it is better to tackle one area at a time. Yes, you can go all in and declutter the entire kitchen in a day or two, but that's not realistic for a lot of people. You have to see what works best with your personal schedule and spend time decluttering accordingly.

For instance, on the first day, you can tackle one or two cabinets, the next day, you can do the cutlery drawers, and so on. There is no right or wrong way of doing this. Whatever fits in with your schedule is the best move for you.

I am often amazed by the things I find stored at the back of my cabinets – so many long-forgotten items that are already long past their shelf life! It is absolutely essential that you get every single item out of the space you are decluttering, clean the space properly (check out the next chapter for my cleaning tips and methods), and then put everything back.

I would recommend that you read the organizing chapter as well to make sure that you are placing everything back in an organized fashion. Alternatively, you can create a temporary storage solution (like placing everything that is supposed to belong in a specific area inside a cardboard box). In that case, you can wait for the next chapters and then follow the instructions for cleaning and organizing everything. This would work well for people who like to do only one thing at a time. So if you want to focus only on the decluttering for now, then place everything in some kind of a temporary storage.

Again, there is no right or wrong way of doing this. You have to take into account your lifestyle and the amount of time you have. If you must maintain a functional kitchen throughout the decluttering and organizing period, then it may be a better idea for you to read the other chapters also right away. For you, decluttering, cleaning, and organizing one area at a time will be a better strategy.

Things to Consider Getting Rid Of

To give you further clarity on which items you should definitely declutter from your kitchen, here are a few pointers.

Gadgets You Don't Use

I absolutely love kitchen gadgets. They make life easier by making cooking more efficient. However, a lot of times, we buy a gadget that is a pain to assemble. It is simply not worth taking it out and putting it together every time we need it for something. As a result, most of the time, the gadget just sits around occupying valuable real estate in the kitchen while a simple tool that can be easily pulled out ends up being frequently used.

I want to urge you to re-evaluate every single gadget you have in your kitchen. Which ones are you really using? How often are you using them? Is it a lot more time and energy efficient to grab a simple tool?

I am suggesting that you get rid of all the gadgets that aren't being used regularly. If you aren't ready to part with them right away, then at least shift them to the ponder box. In case you end up truly missing any of them, you can rescue the gadget and place it back in your kitchen. However, if the idea of rescuing it also feels like a lot of work and you'd much rather just use another tool because it is easier to reach and faster to use, then you definitely don't need that gadget!

Expired Food Items

I know this sounds like a no-brainer but it's amazing how many expired food items I see in people's homes. You want to go check the dates on all cans, spices, and packaged items to find anything that has passed the expiry date. Get rid of these items immediately.

When it comes to food items without an expiry date label, you can check online to get an idea of their shelf life. I would strongly recommend that, moving forward, you write down the date when an item has been added to a container. You can write the date in a subtle manner at the bottom of the container with a marker pen. Every time you refill the container, erase the previous date and write the new one.

Random Lids and Jars

While jars with missing lids can be put to different uses, random lids hardly serve any purpose. I would suggest that you get rid of all the lids that don't match with a container. As for jars and other containers without a lid, see if you can actually put them to good use (like using them as a vase, a pencil holder, a spatula holder, etc.). If not, then get rid of them right away.

Damaged Dishes

Get rid of all chipped china, broken/cracked plates, and damaged glassware. Don't try to think of innovative ways to use them. It is best to purge them right away!

Extra Tools

More often than not, we own far too many kitchen tools. Honestly assess which tools you are actually using and purge the ones that don't get utilized. I know it can be hard to get rid of them as you think you may just need them at some point. Trust me, too many tools only prevent you from accessing the items that you genuinely need.

How many spatulas do you really need and which ones are you actually using? How many egg whisks do you need? Ask yourself this question for every single kitchen tool. Purge or ponder over all the tools that are under-utilized or simply never used.

Too Many Cleaning Supplies

Most of the time, the under-sink area is often a chaotic disaster. Take a look at your cleaning supplies and assess which ones you are really using. Get rid of any expired cleaning products and empty bottles/containers that are still sitting around. Try to pare down your cleaning supplies to the essentials that you are using most of the time.

The Chest Freezer

If you are anything like me, you also probably have a chest freezer where you store frozen food items. I use mine to store food items that I buy in bulk. I keep transferring them to the regular refrigerator freezer once I open them. The chest freezer is where I store my backup food or anything I don't use very frequently, such as ice cream jugs.

Honestly, the chest freezer is often a clutter magnet. It is very easy to overfill it with food that won't ever be used or items that we end up buying too many of simply because they were on sale.

To kickstart the decluttering process, I want you to go through each item that is currently there. Throw away any food item that has gone bad. I know a lot of items in the freezer can be consumed beyond the expiry date, but many times the food just doesn't taste good anymore as it loses flavor and texture. You have to use your discretion to decide if something is still good to be used or not. For example, there have been times when I left frozen pizza in there for too long – alright, I'll admit it, I put it in the freezer and totally forgot it was there. When I tried eating it after a very long time, the crust had become very hard and dry – it tasted like I was eating a styrofoam board.

If you want to be extra safe, then stick with the expiry date on the packet. After all, better safe than sorry! Also, when it comes to ice cream, you should definitely stick to the expiry date on the pack.

In case you have a lot of items that you bought on sale, you may have bought things that you and your family seldom eat. If you find any food item that you never actually consume and you're saving it for a day when you might want to eat such a food item, but you know that's never going to happen, just donate it.

Of course, there is a storage issue here; you can't risk keeping the donation pile sitting around for too long. Ask your neighbor if they have any need for it or immediately drive to the nearest food bank and drop it off there. Resist the temptation of putting it back into the freezer, thinking you'll do this another day. You'll likely end up never doing it. Also, be careful when donating frozen food that is way past the expiry date – others may not be open to receiving it.

You may discover some items that should be in your refrigerator's freezer right now – I know I often forget what I have lying around in the chest freezer. Moving forward, you really need to practice enough self-discipline to cut out the excess that you don't truly need. Discounts are great, but they end up being a waste of money if you are buying too many things you don't need or are never going to use!

Chapter 3

Cleaning the Kitchen

"When your environment is clean you feel happy motivated and healthy."

— *Lailah Gifty Akita (Think Great, Be Great!, 2014)*

Once you have finished decluttering the entire kitchen or a small section of it, it is time to deep clean that space. In this chapter, I am going to give you all the knowledge and instructions you need to clean your kitchen thoroughly. You can start incorporating these cleaning techniques, ideas, and methods into your day-to-day life. The whole point of cleaning regularly is so that you never reach a point when you have so much cleaning to do that it begins to feel like an overwhelming task.

At the end of the chapter, I will share with you good kitchen hygiene habits that you should definitely incorporate into your life. Your kitchen isn't just a space for preparing food; it is the hub of your home – the center from where you and all your family members derive their nourishment. This space should be treated with utmost respect and should be as efficiently functional as possible.

Prepare a Cleaning Caddy

You don't want to have to search all over the place to gather all your cleaning supplies every time you need them. Having all your cleaning supplies neatly stored in a caddy can cut down cleaning time further. You can easily gather all your supplies and get down to business whenever need be.

Also, I strongly believe in aesthetics combined with functionality. Who wants to reach for that ugly blue bucket and rotting sponge – that kind of thing makes your heart sink! You start thinking of cleaning as some kind of punishment. Make your cleaning caddy look as pretty as possible. I would suggest decanting the cleaning supplies into clear bottles. You can label them with chalkboard marker stickers that can be easily bought at any crafts store or online. Try to make your cleaning rags and gloves color coordinated.

I have managed to create a cleaning caddy that is a delight to look at. I would strongly advise that you keep your cleaning tools and supplies stored together in a caddy that can easily be carried around. You can easily buy a caddy with handles online or at your local home goods store. Now, let us discuss in detail the essentials that should be there in your cleaning caddy.

Microfiber Cloths

If you haven't yet gotten your hands on microfiber cloths, then you must acquire them right away! These soft rags act like mini-vacuum cleaners. They are extremely efficient at picking up dust from the surfaces they come in contact with. They work efficiently whether they are used wet or dry.

Cleaning Gloves

That's a no-brainer! We all know that cleaning can take a heavy toll on your hands. Use gloves for all cleaning tasks. You can also apply some heavy hand cream before placing your hands in the gloves. This will allow the moisture to seep much deeper into your skin while you are busy scrubbing the place.

Toothbrushes

Toothbrushes are an indispensable tool in any cleaning kit. You can buy them inexpensively at the local discount store. Just make sure that you are buying the soft-bristled ones. Keep separate toothbrushes for different cleaning jobs. You can label each one with a permanent marker. In my case, I have a dedicated brush for polishing silver, another one for cleaning around bathroom faucets, a separate toothbrush for scrubbing the kitchen faucet, and so on.

Cleaning Products

You don't need too many different types of cleansers. All you need is one glass cleaner and one multi-purpose cleaner. You can make your own DIY glass cleaner by mixing one cup of white vinegar with one cup of water and one cup of rubbing alcohol. For the all-purpose cleaner, skip the alcohol and mix one cup of white vinegar with one cup of water. You can also add a few drops of your favorite essential oil to the mix.

Cloths and Rags

Separate cloths and rags should be used for different kitchen cleaning purposes. A few rags should be set aside for cleaning up spills and washing the floors.

You should also have a few cloths and rags set aside for extremely dirty jobs. For instance, you can have a few for cleaning up nasty spills. Don't worry about keeping these rags and cloths stain-free.

Other Essential Kitchen Supplies

Apart from the cleaning caddy, you also need dishcloths in the kitchen for drying dishes and for wiping sinks, countertops, and tabletops. Make sure that you keep a separate dishcloth for each job. Hand towels should also be kept around to wipe hands while performing tasks.

Fine linen can be used for drying and polishing glassware, china, crystal, and silver. Make sure you have plenty of towels, cloths, and rags in your kitchen for all these different purposes. They should not be thrown in with the regular laundry. You can run your cleaning supplies in a separate load. If possible, don't wash the cloths, rags, and towels you have set aside for heavy-duty tasks with the ones that are meant for light cleaning purposes.

Start Cleaning

After completely decluttering a space, you must take the time to clean it thoroughly. Wipe all shelves, baseboard, cupboard doors, and other surfaces with the all-purpose cleaner using a microfiber cloth. Once the surfaces are dry, wipe them again with a dry cloth to ensure no dirt or debris remains.

Clean the kitchen windows and doors. Don't forget to wipe doorknobs and door handles, as well. Again, wipe first with a wet cloth and then, later on, with a dry cloth. Vacuum the floors and then use a wet mop to remove any dirt that may remain behind. Microfiber mops are much more efficient at cleaning than regular mops.

Cleaning the Dishes

Before you get to organizing your dishes, you must clean them thoroughly (especially the ones that haven't been used in a while). If you are washing the dishes by hand, then start with those dishes that are least soiled, and then progress on to the most heavily soiled ones. This means you would likely begin with glass, silver, and flatware. Be sure to use hot, sudsy water to clean the dishes.

To prevent breakage, wash similar items together. Glasses and plates, for example, should be washed separately from heavy pots and pans. For delicate or valuable items, wash only one item at a time.

If you want to wash the dishes in the dishwasher, then be sure to scrape off any hardened food debris that may be stuck on them. I would strongly recommend that you rinse all dishes before placing them in the dishwasher. This prevents utensils from aging prematurely; they won't get damaged by the excess friction caused by food particles flying around in the dishwasher.

You also want to place delicate and heat-vulnerable items on the top rack of the dishwasher and never on the lower rack. Follow the instructions on the dishwasher's user manual to prevent damaging your dishes and dishwasher.

Cleaning the Refrigerator

This is one area of the kitchen that often doesn't receive as much attention as it deserves. Since fresh food is stored in the refrigerator, there's always a chance of germs accumulating due to accidental spills, spoiled food, developing mold, etc.

Go through all the contents of your refrigerator (including the freezer and the vegetable drawer) and throw away anything that has gone bad. Get rid of any rotting piece of fruit or vegetable. One rotten piece can ruin the entire bunch.

Remove the shelves and drawers of the refrigerator. Club highly perishable items together and place them on one or two shelves that you leave inside the refrigerator. Place the remaining (not highly perishable) food items on the kitchen countertop.

Wash the shelves and drawers thoroughly with hot soapy water. Rinse and dry them. Wipe the surface of the refrigerator where they will be placed and then place them back. Shift the highly perishable items to the clean shelves and wash the shelf they had been standing on.

Don't use hot water on cold glass shelves – they may crack. Use any all-purpose cleaner to wipe the surfaces clean. For deodorizing the refrigerator, you can use baking soda. Add two tablespoons of baking soda to 500ml water and use the mixture to wipe the refrigerator surfaces.

Use these same suggestions to clean the freezer and chest freezer if you own one. Just make sure that you defrost the freezer, following the manufacturer's instructions, prior to the deep cleaning. If you have two freezers, then you can transfer as many food items to the other freezer as possible while doing the cleaning. Alternatively, you can preserve the food in an ice chest while cleaning the freezer.

Cleaning Stoves and Ovens

If you have a gas stove, remove the burner pans and burner grates. In the case of an electric stove, remove the heating elements and the reflector bowls underneath them. Soak the burner pans/grates/reflector bowls (except the heating elements of an electric stove) in a mixture of hot water and dishwashing liquid. After 15-20 minutes, wash them thoroughly and set them aside to dry. The heating elements need only be wiped with a well-wrung damp cloth (make sure that you are wiping them only when they are completely cool).

Wipe the stovetop with a solution of hot water and liquid detergent. If there are any stubborn food particles stuck on the stove surface, you can dampen them and allow them to stand until they soften. Once the stove is completely clean, replace the burner pans, grates, and reflector bowls. Wipe the exterior of the oven door and other accessible parts of the stovetop with the same mixture.

Most ovens these days have a self-cleaning mechanism. Don't use detergent inside the oven or you could end up destroying the self-cleaning mechanism of the oven surfaces. For cleaning the oven properly, it's best to follow the instruction manual that came with it. In case you have a non-self-cleaning oven, it would be best to buy a commercial oven cleaner and use it as advised by the manufacturer.

The broiling pan used in the oven is often safe for dishwashers and can be cleaned in the same way you would clean a soiled pan.

Cleaning the Microwave

Commercial oven cleaners should never be used inside a microwave. Use a cloth dipped in warm, sudsy water (any mild liquid detergent will work) to wipe off all surfaces. Be sure to wipe all surfaces, including the top, bottom, sides, and both sides of the door. Clean the door seals and seams as well.

Daily Kitchen Cleaning Routine and Habits to Incorporate

- Clean and tidy the kitchen as you are cooking. Don't leave it for when you finish cooking.
- Wash ALL the dishes – load the dishes in the dishwasher and/or hand wash them before going to bed.
- Clean the sink after each use (using warm water and dishwashing liquid). Wipe the sink with a cloth dedicated for that purpose – your goal should be a fresh, sparkling, dry sink at all times.
- Every morning, or as soon as the dishes have dried, place them back in their spot.
- Wipe kitchen countertops and stovetops (wipe the burners and baskets without removing them).
- Sweep kitchen floor.
- Wipe the kitchen table.
- Change kitchen towels daily.
- Clean all spills immediately – don't allow them to dry up.
- Throw away anything in the refrigerator that has turned moldy, smelly, spotty, or slimy.
- Take the trash out.

Weekly Kitchen Cleaning Routine

- Go through all the contents of the refrigerator (best done immediately or a day before the weekly grocery shopping).
- Wash the refrigerator.
- Take burner pans and burner grates off gas stoves to clean them thoroughly.
- Launder all kitchen cloths, towels, and rags.
- Clean all other kitchen appliances.
- Sanitize your sponges – microwave them on high heat for one minute.
- Mop the kitchen floor.
- Wipe all cabinet doors and handles.
- Wipe kitchen door, windows, and handles.
- Clean the garbage disposal unit (follow manufacturer's instructions).

Monthly Kitchen Cleaning Routine

- Deep clean all cabinets, cupboards, and drawers.
- Go through all pantry items – discard all expired food.
- Clean and sanitize trash/recycling bins.
- Deep clean the dishwasher (follow manufacturer's instructions).
- Wash kitchen rugs (if you have any).
- Dust and wipe all light fixtures.

Lisa Hedberg

To Be Done When Needed Kitchen Cleaning Routine

- Deep clean the oven.
- Clean under the refrigerator.
- Declutter, clean, and organize all kitchen tools.
- Repair or replace damaged tools as needed.
- Defrost and deep clean the freezer.

Chapter 4

Organizing the Kitchen

"Being organized isn't about getting rid of everything you own or trying to become a different person: it's about living the way you want to live, but better."

— *Andrew Mellen (Thought for Today - Organization, n.d.)*

Now that you have finished decluttering and cleaning, it's time to start organizing the kitchen! Again, if you have a large kitchen or you're simply short on time, then you want to complete this task bit-by-bit, tackling one small area at a time.

If you are doing the entire kitchen in one go, then it's best, I would say, that you begin the organization project with your refrigerator. This is so that you can put back all perishable items immediately.

Lisa Hedberg

Refrigerator

The open shelving space inside the refrigerator can quickly turn into a total disaster zone if you aren't intentional with your organizing. Moving forward, don't store anything randomly. Every item should belong to a category, and there should be a container for storing items belonging to that category.

You want to invest in good-quality clear plastic bins designed specifically for the refrigerator. An ordinary organizer won't do the job; you want to make sure that the material can withstand constant cold temperatures inside the refrigerator.

These organizer bins come in a host of different shapes and sizes. You can buy several different shapes and sizes for variety. To maximize the vertical space inside the refrigerator, you can also buy sliding drawers that can easily be attached to the shelf. You might also get a drawer that is designed specifically for eggs in case you have a lot of eggs to store.

These clear containers can be used for versatile purposes. For instance, one week, you may use a bin to store fresh fruits and another week for keeping your leftover turkey sandwich safe. You also want to store together items that you would use at the same time. For example, store sandwich ingredients together (in other words, club together the meat, sauces/spreads, and cheese) so that you can easily assemble a sandwich without having to rummage through the entire refrigerator for 10-15 minutes.

The key to an organized refrigerator lies in limiting the open shelf space. Only those items that are too large and bulky to be stored in any of the bins should be stored in the open shelf space. A large milk or juice jug may not fit anywhere else.

Similarly, if you are storing pre-cut vegetables in large jars, they might fit better in the open shelf space.

To make your refrigerator more aesthetically pleasing, I would suggest getting rid of food packaging. Store everything in clear glass or plastic containers. You can use dishwasher-safe chalkboard labels (easily available online or at any local crafts store) to note down the item name and the expiry date.

Here are some more tips for making your refrigerator more organized and aesthetically pleasing:

- Use stackable wine racks for storing wine bottles.
- Use waterproof refrigerator mats to line the shelves and drawers of your refrigerator (this will make cleaning a lot easier as you can remove the mats and wash them separately – no need to remove the shelves and drawers every week. You can clean them once every couple of months by taking everything out).
- Store leftovers in glass storage boxes.

Again, minimizing the packaging material is the best way to make your refrigerator look neat and attractive. Your refrigerator should be a delightful sight to behold every time you open the door.

How to Utilize the Shelves and Drawers in Your Refrigerator

The top shelf is the warmest shelf in your refrigerator. Use it for storing leftovers, snacks, and other items that you intend to eat soon. Don't use it for storing fresh meat.

The middle shelf enjoys consistently cooler temperatures. Use it for storing items that are likely to spoil easily. For instance, milk and eggs. Since this shelf usually has the maximum amount of vertical shelving space, it can be used for storing taller containers.

The bottom shelf is the coolest spot in your refrigerator. Use it for storing meat and other items that must be kept at consistently low temperatures.

The bottom drawers are usually dedicated to storing fruits and vegetables. Just make sure you are storing fruits and vegetables separately because the ethylene emitted by fruits can cause vegetables to spoil prematurely.

The door is the warmest part of your refrigerator. You should definitely not store eggs here. It is ideal for storing condiments that are high in salt and/or vinegar. You can also store jams and jellies here.

Freezer and Chest Freezer

If you aren't using some kind of an organizer in the freezer, then you are guaranteed to end up with a jumbled mess. I personally love using freezer-safe clear boxes to keep similar items together. I would strongly recommend that you label each box. You can stack them on top of one another.

In the case of the chest freezer, you can also use crates, baskets, or maybe even cardboard boxes (if you are on a budget). The point is to create a clear demarcation of space and keep similar things grouped with items in the same category.

Another very important thing for keeping the freezer organized is to maintain an inventory. Keep stock of exactly what items are stored in the freezer and the chest freezer. Every time you pull something out of either of the two, update the inventory. If you are moving something from the chest freezer to the refrigerator's freezer, then that needs to be updated accordingly as well. This will help you keep track of the items you currently have and what you are running low on. That way, you'll be able to restock it in a timely manner.

Each of your freezers should have a separate inventory. Train your family to update the inventory every time they pull something out of the freezer, as well.

Pantry

Your pantry should be organized in such a way that you can quickly put away groceries after returning from the store. Everything should be clearly visible and easily accessible; that way, you don't have to figure out what's inside which container.

I would advise you to measure your pantry space (both the length and the width) to know the exact dimensions you're working with. Don't skip this step – it will really help out with planning your pantry layout. Knowing the exact dimensions of your space will help you determine the size and number of organizers you need in it.

Write down the different sections you need to create for separate categories of food. For instance, you can have sections like ready-to-eat snacks, breakfast cereals, baking goods, etc. How many sections you need to create in your pantry will depend entirely upon your unique needs. To decide which sections you need, you can also run through an entire day in your head – see what you and your family are eating throughout the course of the day.

Once you have decided the number of sections you need and you're familiar with the total pantry area available to you, it's time to select your storage containers. Take into consideration the total number of items you generally have for each category of food, and then create an estimate for the number of jars, bins, and baskets you are going to need.

I am a strong proponent of using clear containers in the pantry. Getting rid of the original packaging in which the food comes is essential for making your pantry look aesthetically pleasing. Besides, when everything is placed inside clear containers, you can easily see exactly what items you have available. I recommend writing the expiry date for each item at the bottom of the clear container. You can use a marker pen that can easily be erased using a glass cleaner.

If you want to make your pantry look like the ones from home decor magazines, it's best that you store only one size and style of storage containers in each area. For example, you can store all your rice and beans in one section using glass jars that are the same size and height. This makes everything look very uniform and neat.

To keep all the containers visible, you can place the ones at the back of the shelf on a wooden block. Use wooden blocks to create separate rows of containers so they can be visible according to their cascading height – the tallest ones at the back should be raised the highest. The ones in front of them should be slightly lower, and the height of the blocks should descend consistently. The front row containers should be placed directly on the shelf and should be the lowest ones in the order of height.

To make the food items even easier to access, you can label the containers. Use a label maker to create professional-looking labels. Alternatively, you can buy chalkboard stickers and manually label each container.

Spices

I personally like to use a drawer organizer for storing all my spices in alphabetical order. I write the expiry date at the bottom of each jar. If you have a drawer that you can dedicate to spices, then you can buy a tiered rack that would fit into the drawer.

You can also install a wall-mounted rack or a sliding spice rack inside your cabinet. Some people also like to store their spices on a lazy Susan style of organizer. There are indeed many options available in the market. You can get one that suits your space and your style the best.

Again, storing the spices and herbs in the same size/type of containers helps keep everything looking neat. The labeling should also be consistent – use the same type and style of labeling to make sure everything looks uniform.

Cooking Tools and Serving Utensils

It can be hard to find the right cooking tool when you have an overabundance of utensils. I hope you took the decluttering aspect very seriously and have now pared down to the tools you actually use. I like to store my cooking tools close to the stove so that I can grab what I need easily while preparing food. The tools I don't use that often (like baking tools) are stored in another drawer that is less easily accessible. Serving utensils are stored in another drawer that is also close to the stove so I can quickly grab the right tools when I am getting ready to serve the food.

I like using expandable drawer organizers for storing cooking tools, serving utensils, and cutlery. You can get them in plastic or bamboo material. I personally prefer the bamboo organizer. You can also get a utensil holder for storing your kitchen tools near the stovetop. I like to keep my countertop as clean and uncluttered as possible. Hence, I prefer storing everything in closed drawers, cabinets, and cupboards.

Pots and Pans

I know that most people just stack pots and pans on top of one another. I personally detest this as I have to dig out the one I need every time I'm cooking. Also, this method causes a lot of wear and tear to your utensils. I would recommend investing in pots and pans organizer racks that can easily be stored inside cabinets. It's not a huge space saver, but it does help elongate the life of your utensils. It also makes pulling out the right pot or pan very easy and convenient.

I like to keep the lid and pot or pan together. This way, I can pull both of them out in one go. May not seem like much, but as a busy mother and wife, I'm grateful for even the smallest amount of time I manage to save throughout the day!

Dishes

I like to store my plates in vertical plate holders. I stack smaller plates together and larger plates as a separate section of their own. I place bowls of the same size one on top of the other. To maximize the shelf space in cabinets, I use shelf racks. This way, I can organize mugs, bowls, and other dishes in a tiered fashion.

Depending upon the type of space available to you, you can go two ways. Get a shelf rack that can be placed anywhere in the cabinet or even on the countertop if you wish. Or you can get a two-tiered corner shelf rack that will help maximize the corner space you have available.

For wine glasses, you can buy an under-cabinet wine glass holder shelf. This way, all the glasses are easily accessible while occupying limited space in your kitchen cabinets. When it comes to storing glasses without a stem, you can place them on the shelf, or you can store them on a glass drying rack.

Kitchen Gadgets

I know how tempting it is to buy lots of different gadgets. But, to be honest, the idea that they make life easier for you is something of an illusion. Most people have too many gadgets that they never use. I would suggest that you pare down to the bare essentials – keep only those gadgets around that you use regularly.

Again, I am not a fan of storing things on the kitchen countertop. I like to store my gadgets in organizer bins inside closed cabinets. The gadgets that you rarely use but are not ready to part with can be stored away from the cooking area on the top shelf of a cabinet at the back.

I hope you enjoyed all the kitchen organization hacks I shared with you in this chapter. Organization shouldn't be something that you do only once and then forget about. You have to regularly keep repeating the process of decluttering, cleaning, and organizing. That's especially true when we are talking about a space that is as dynamic as the kitchen. You also don't have to get everything on point right away. Over time, you can further refine your system and become more organized – just do what you are able to do right now because that is good enough!

Chapter 5
Meal Planning

"View health as an investment, not an expense."

— *John Quelch (BrainyQuote, n.d.)*

If you want to do anything well in life, you need a plan for exactly how you'll go about it. Hence, if you want to feed wholesome, nourishing food to yourself and your family, then you need to plan all your meals ahead of time. After all, standing in front of the refrigerator wondering what you can cook this evening isn't the most productive use of time. Worse still, you may start preparing a meal and then realize you are short on several ingredients. We have all been through that nightmare when we drove to the grocery store just to get one key ingredient that was missing from our repertoire, only to come back home and realize that we need to run back to the store to get another ingredient we don't have at hand!

Lisa Hedberg

Creating a Meal Plan

I generally go through all my refrigerator items once a week. I also try to wash and wipe all the shelf liners and organizer baskets after removing any food item that's gone bad. While I am doing the culling, I am also noting down the items I need to restock. By the end of the refrigerator purge, I have a list of items that need to be bought for the week.

Once I am done with the refrigerator, I sit down to create a menu plan for the week. I know there are many kinds of fancy planners available for it these days, but I use a regular notebook to write down what I am planning to prepare for breakfast, lunch, and dinner each day of the week. You can also do this digitally if you prefer, but I prefer to write things on paper the old-fashioned way. It helps me to think more clearly, and I simply tend to plan better on paper.

After preparing the menu for the week, I write down the ingredients that would be needed for each meal, marking anything that is currently not available in my kitchen. You don't have to write the ingredient list every single time. What I realized is that I prepare the same kind of dishes in rotation. I have prepared a separate recipe card for each dish. I refer to this card and make note of any ingredient that is currently not available in my kitchen. All such items get added to my grocery shopping list for the week.

If you don't want to prepare a meal plan for the entire week, then you can also do it for the next 2-3 days or whatever works best for you. For me and for most people, planning everything in one go for the entire week works better. I am able to do my grocery shopping once a week, and one trip to the market proves sufficient to supply me with all the essentials for that week. If you're going to do the meal planning every couple of days, then you'll also have to factor in more visits to the grocery store since you're likely going to be short on at least some of the ingredients required for the meals.

Shopping for Food

I like to patronize the same shops in my locality frequently. Over time, I have managed to develop a rapport with the staff there, so they're better able to assist me with my needs. I am also well familiar with all the shelves and sections in those shops, so I don't waste much time when I go there.

While shopping, it is best to start with non-perishable items like canned, bottled, and any other packaged item that doesn't need to be stored in the refrigerator or freezer. That would include items like breakfast cereals, rice, beans, pasta, etc. Next up, I like to stock up on refrigerated items like cheese, meat, poultry, milk, fruits, vegetables, etc.

At the very end, I load up my cart with any frozen food or hot cooked item that I may be buying. Make sure that you aren't picking any frozen food that has been left lying above the freezer line where there's a chance of it going bad. It also goes without saying (but I'll say it anyway!) that you want to carefully check the packaging and expiry date of each item before placing it in your cart.

You should also ensure that you are placing all the items in your cart according to their temperature. So, for instance, items at room temperature should be grouped together, cold/frozen items should be placed near each other, and any hot food should be kept with other hot items only.

Lisa Hedberg

During the bagging process, make sure that the hot and cold items are bagged separately. Meats, poultry, and any other food item that may drip raw juices or liquids should be placed inside an extra layer of plastic bag. This way, the drips won't fall on other food items. Avoid buying packets that are dripping in the first place, but if it starts happening after you have made the purchase, placing them inside an additional plastic bag is your best bet.

If you are planning to run other errands on the same day that you go grocery shopping, try to shop for food at the end of your trip. Post-grocery shopping, try to get back home as fast as possible. When the weather is hot, place the groceries in the passenger area of your car and keep the air conditioner switched on. If you must take a detour before coming back home, then you can take a portable ice chest with you before heading out to the grocery store.

Put food away right after you return from the store. Be sure to tackle hot, frozen, or cold food items first. Store them at the appropriate temperature.

Note: I want to include a word of caution here. Thanks to the overabundance of food in our 'modern' lives, it can be tempting to buy more food than we need, especially if we find something on sale. Don't get me wrong – I am myself obsessed with finding great bargains and discounts, but I have had to learn to draw the line. It is tempting to buy ten boxes of strawberries because they are for sale at $1 each, but what's the point if I can't finish them and they start going bad by the following day? If you think about it, instead of being a money saver, such a fear actually ends up as a significant waste.

Besides, when you buy things like microwaveable pizza on sale, you feel obliged to finish all of it even though you already started feeling full after two slices. You can end up overeating by consuming excess calories simply because you didn't want to waste the pizza and you think you should get your money's worth.

I want you to start being more disciplined with your purchases. Don't buy things you or your family are unlikely to eat within their expiry period just because they're on sale. Stick to your original grocery list that you prepared after creating your weekly meal plan. It will help you remain focused. In the long run, you'll eat healthier and save more money. A lot of bargains are not really bargains when you factor in their long-term impact on your health and wallet. But if you find something at a bargain price that you will definitely be eating (and you are sure it will be consumed within its expiration period), then by all means go for it!

Meal Prep in Advance

You can save time by prepping for the next day's meal while cooking dinner the night before. This could mean chopping the onions, peeling the cucumbers or carrots, and mixing the marinade for the chicken. Whatever kind of meal it will be, start preparing for it as much in advance as possible.

You can classify one area of your refrigerator as the meal prep section. You can use a refrigerator-safe tray for separating this section. This is where you'll store all the prepped items. I like to use clear click-and-lock style food containers for all the chopped vegetables and fruits. For liquids, I like to use mason jars. I would advise you to get containers in different sizes to accommodate the various quantities of prepped items your recipes may require.

When you have prepped in advance, it is a lot easier to do the cooking when mealtime approaches. No matter how tired you are, you can find some energy to cook when all the toughest jobs have already been dealt with.

Conclusion

I hope you have enjoyed reading this book as much as I have loved writing it. I hope you have taken all the action steps I have highlighted throughout this book and now you are able to enjoy a kitchen that is functional while also being aesthetically pleasing.

If you haven't done everything, then go back to chapter 1 and start the process all over again. You can do it! I believe in you – you must also believe in yourself. Slowly, one step at a time, you'll get to the final destination.

Lastly, I want to remind you that decluttering, cleaning, and organizing are not things we do once in a while. To live a beautiful life, we must incorporate these three into our daily routines. They should feel more like a natural way of life than tasks to be accomplished within a certain time frame.

It you want to learn more about decluttering, check out my my book, *Decluttering Workbook: The Essential Guide to Organize and Declutter Your Home and Life With Exercises and Checklists.*

Conclusion

Once again, thank you for placing your trust in me. Wishing you a beautiful kitchen, a lovely home, and great health for the rest of your life!

Lisa

Thank You

Thank you for purchasing my book.

You chose this book. Thank you for picking it! And thanks for reading it all the way through. I hope you received value from the book and found the decluttering advice to be helpful.

Could you please consider writing a review of my book on the platform?

Writing a review is the best and easiest way to support people like me who self-publish books. Your review helps other people find my work and enjoy it, too!

It will help me write the kind of books that will help you get the results you want. It would mean a lot to me to hear from you.

>> **Leave a review on Amazon US** <<
>> **Leave a review on Amazon UK** <<

References

Akita, L. G. (2014). *Think Great, Be Great!* (Vol. 1). CreateSpace Independent Publishing Platform; Edition 1.

Becker, J. (n.d.). *Joshua Becker*. Goodreads. Retrieved May 10, 2022, from https://www.goodreads.com/quotes/7048262-the-first-step-in-crafting-the-life-you-want-is

Benjamin Franklin. BrainyQuote. (n.d.). Retrieved May 10, 2022, from https://www.brainyquote.com/quotes/benjamin_franklin_138217

Hicks, D. C. (2020, November). *Understanding well-being: Clearing Personal Space For Wellness*. Harvard Library Office for Scholarly Communication. Retrieved May 10, 2022, from https://dash.harvard.edu/handle/1/37365612

Mellen, A. (n.d.). *Thought for Today - Organization*. Oprah.com. Retrieved May 10, 2022, from https://www.oprah.com/spirit/thought-for-today-quotes-on-organization/all

References

Quelch, J. (n.d.). *John Quelch quotes*. BrainyQuote. Retrieved May 10, 2022, from https://www.brainyquote.com/quotes/john_quelch_757984

www.ingramcontent.com/pod-product-compliance
Lightning Source LLC
Chambersburg PA
CBHW030311100526
44590CB00012B/600